Crispy Chicken Wings Recipes

Enjoy Delish, Crispy Chicken Wings in No Time!

BY: GRACE BERRY

Copyright © 2020 by Grace Berry. All Rights Reserved.

www.graceberry.net

License Notes

This book is an informational material. The author has taken great care to ensure the correctness of the content. However, the reader assumes all responsibility of how the information is used, and the author shall not be accountable for any form of misuse or misinterpretation on the part of the reader.

All rights reserved. On no account may any part of the material be copied, reproduced, or distributed in any form without written permission from the author.

Table of Contents

Introduction 6

    Grilled Chicken Wings 7

    Honey Garlic Chicken Wings 9

    Spicy Asian Chicken Wings 11

    Classic BBQ Chicken Wings 13

    Bacon-Wrapped Chicken Wings 15

    Lemon Herb Grilled Chicken Wings 17

    Spicy Grilled Chicken Wings 19

    Classic Buffalo Wings 21

    Barbecue Bourbon Chicken Wings 23

    Crispy Fried Chicken Wings 25

    Sweet Chili Glazed BBQ Chicken Wings 27

    Spicy Maple Chicken Wings 30

    Garlic Parmesan Chicken Wings 32

Boozy Chicken Wings 34

Chili Lime Beer Chicken Wings 36

Cilantro Lime Wings 38

Jerk Chicken Wings 40

Pineapple Chicken Wings 42

Super Spicy Chicken Wings 44

Baked Chicken Wings 46

Lemon Pepper Chicken Wings 48

Honey-Lime Chicken Wings 50

Balsamic Glazed Wings 52

Italian Style Grilled Chicken Wings 54

Spicy Jalapeno Grilled Chicken Wings 56

Jack Daniel's Barbecue Wings 59

Honey Barbecue Chicken Wings 61

Cherry Barbecue Chicken Wings 63

Chicken Parm Wings 65

Honey Balsamic Grilled Chicken Wings 67

Conclusion 70

Author's Afterthoughts 71

About the Author 72

Introduction

Wings are not only convenient and able to feed a bunch of people, but they are packed with finger licking delicious flavors. You can grab some spices from your spice rack and a few sauces and make some chicken wing magic! For grill recipes, you can use an indoor grill pan or an outdoor grill.

Chicken wings go great with any sides, but I personally recommend some classic French fries. Grab your spicy barbecue sauce or cool ranch dressing and let's go!

Grilled Chicken Wings

These grilled wings are great for huge gatherings because everybody can just choose the sauce they want. Have a couple of different sauce options ready for people to enjoy these delicately seasoned wings with.

Prep Time: 30 minutes

Serving: 6

Ingredients:

- 3 pounds chicken wings, washed and patted dry
- ¼ cup olive oil
- 2 tablespoons brown sugar
- 2 tablespoons soy sauce
- 1 tablespoon garlic powder
- 1 tablespoon dried thyme
- 1 teaspoon lemon zest
- 1 teaspoon salt
- ½ teaspoon cayenne
- 1 teaspoon black pepper

Instructions:

1. In a medium bowl, mix together olive oil, brown sugar, soy sauce, garlic powder, thyme, lemon zest, salt, cayenne and black pepper.

2. To marinate chicken wings, place them in a large bowl or a resealable bag with the olive oil mixture. Marinate for at least 20 minutes.

3. Heat your outdoor or indoor grill to medium heat.

4. Add wings to the grill and cook for about 10 minutes each side, until wings are cooked and crisp.

Honey Garlic Chicken Wings

These juicy chicken wings will tantalize your taste buds. The sweet honey caramel over the wings and go great with the delicious garlic flavor.

Prep Time: 35 minutes

Serving: 6

Ingredients:

- 3 pounds chicken wings, washed and patted dry
- 2 teaspoons of red pepper flakes
- 1 tablespoon chicken seasoning
- 1 teaspoon salt
- 6 garlic cloves, minced
- 1 tablespoon ginger, minced
- ¼ cup honey
- 1 teaspoon brown sugar
- 2 tablespoons water

Instructions:

1. Preheat your oven to 450 degrees F.

2. Toss wings with red pepper flakes, salt and chicken seasoning and place on a parchment lined baking sheet.

3. Bake wings for 20 minutes and flip them half way through (10 minutes).

4. While your wings are baking, add garlic, ginger, honey, brown sugar and water to a skillet. Cook on low heat until sauce has reduced and thickened.

5. Once wings are ready, remove them from the oven and add to the sauce.

6. Cook over medium heat until sauce has stuck to the wings.

Spicy Asian Chicken Wings

These flavorful crispy wings are filled with wonderful layers of flavor. From garlic to ginger to soy sauce all mixed together with chili garlic sauce.

Prep Time: 50 minutes

Serving: 6

Ingredients:

- 3 pounds chicken wings, washed and patted dry
- ½ cup low sodium soy sauce
- ¼ cup olive oil
- ¼ cup chili garlic sauce
- ¼ cup honey
- 5 garlic cloves, minced
- 1 tablespoon ginger, minced
- 1 tablespoon lime juice

Instructions:

1. Mix together soy sauce, olive oil, chili garlic sauce, honey, garlic, lime juice and ginger. Save ½ cup of the mixture to be used as a glaze.

2. Toss wings with the remaining of the mixture and marinate for at least 20 minutes.

3. Preheat your oven to 450 degrees F.

4. Place wings on a wire rack and bake wings for 30 - 40 minutes, turning them half way through.

5. While your wings are baking, add the other half of the sauce to a skillet and cook on low heat until sauce has reduced and thickened.

6. Once wings are ready, remove them from the oven and add to the sauce.

7. Cook over medium heat until sauce has stuck to the wings.

Classic BBQ Chicken Wings

These baked barbecue chicken wings are deliciously smothered in sweet and tangy barbecue sauce. No need to order wings for your next game day!

Prep Time: 30 minutes

Serving: 6

Ingredients:

- 3 pounds chicken wings, washed and patted dry
- 1 ½ cups of barbecue sauce
- ¼ cup ketchup
- 2 teaspoons brown sugar
- 1 tablespoon chicken seasoning
- 1 teaspoon salt
- ½ teaspoon black pepper
- 2 tablespoons water

Instructions:

1. Preheat your oven to 450 degrees F.

2. Toss wings with olive oil, salt, black pepper and chicken seasoning and place on a parchment lined baking sheet.

3. Bake wings for 20 minutes and flip them half way through (10 minutes).

4. While your wings are baking, add brown sugar, barbecue sauce, ketchup and water to a skillet. Cook on low heat until sauce has reduced and thickened.

5. Once wings are ready, remove them from the oven and add to the sauce.

6. Cook over medium heat until sauce has stuck to the wings.

Bacon-Wrapped Chicken Wings

Spiced chicken wings are even tastier when they are wrapped in salty, crispy bacon.

Prep Time: 40 minutes

Serving: 6

Ingredients:

- 24 chicken wings
- 24 strips of bacon
- 1 teaspoon salt
- ½ teaspoon black pepper
- 1 teaspoon chicken seasoning
- ½ teaspoon paprika
- 1 teaspoon chili powder
- 1 tablespoon brown sugar
- 2 teaspoons oregano

Instructions:

1. Preheat the oven to 450 degrees F. Season chicken wings with salt, black pepper, chicken seasoning, paprika, chili powder, brown sugar and oregano.

2. Carefully wrap each wing with a strip of bacon and place on a baking rack over a baking sheet lined with foil.

3. Bake wings for about 35 - 40 minutes, until cooked through. Turning half way through.

Lemon Herb Grilled Chicken Wings

These grilled chicken wings are fresh and filled with flavor. They're seasoning with a delicious combination of herbs and spices tied together with fresh lemon juice.

Prep Time: 30 minutes

Serving: 6

Ingredients:

- 3 pounds chicken wings, washed and patted dry
- 1 teaspoon salt
- ½ teaspoon black pepper
- 3 cloves garlic, minced
- ½ teaspoon cayenne pepper
- ½ teaspoon paprika
- 1 tablespoon dried thyme leaves
- 1 tablespoon dried Italian seasoning
- 2 tablespoons fresh cilantro, chopped
- 2 tablespoons lemon juice
- ½ cup olive oil

Instructions:

1. In a large bowl, mix together olive oil, salt, black pepper, garlic, cayenne, paprika, thyme, Italian seasoning, lemon juice and cilantro in a bowl.

2. Add chicken to the bowl and allow to marinate for at least 20 minutes.

3. Heat your outdoor or indoor grill to medium heat.

4. Add wings to the grill and cook for about 10 minutes each side, until wings are cooked and crisp.

Spicy Grilled Chicken Wings

Let's kick up the heat with these spicy grilled chicken wings. These are an amazing combination of dried spices and hot sauce.

Prep Time: 30 minutes

Serving: 6

Ingredients:

- 3 pounds of chicken wings, washed and patted dry
- ¼ teaspoon salt
- ¼ teaspoon black pepper
- 1 teaspoon cayenne
- 1 teaspoon paprika
- 1 teaspoon red pepper flakes
- 1 teaspoon garlic powder
- ½ cup of hot sauce
- ¼ cup olive oil

Instructions:

1. To make the spicy marinade, in a small bowl combine salt, pepper, cayenne, paprika, red pepper flakes, garlic powder and hot sauce.

2. Add chicken to a large bowl, toss with olive oil and spicy marinade and allow to marinate for 15 minutes.

3. Heat grill to medium heat and grill chicken until cooked and slightly charred, about 10 minutes on each side.

Classic Buffalo Wings

Grab your ranch dressing, it's time to enjoy a heat filled classic!

Prep Time: 30 minutes

Serving: 6

Ingredients:

- 3 pounds of chicken wings, washed and patted dry
- ¼ teaspoon salt
- ¼ teaspoon black pepper
- 2 teaspoons garlic powder
- ½ cup of hot sauce
- ¼ cup honey
- 4 tablespoons butter
- ¼ cup olive oil

Instructions:

1. Preheat your oven to 450 degrees F.

2. Toss wings with olive oil, salt, black pepper and garlic powder and place on a parchment lined baking sheet.

3. Bake wings for 20 - 30 minutes until crispy and flip them half way through (10 minutes).

4. While your wings are baking, add hot sauce and honey to a small saucepan, bring to a simmer and then add butter. Cook on low heat until sauce has reduced and thickened.

5. Once wings are ready, remove them from the oven and add to the sauce.

6. Cook over medium heat until sauce has stuck to the wings

Barbecue Bourbon Chicken Wings

Step your barbecue wings up with a little bourbon. We make these fall off the bone wings in a slow cooker. Just set them and forget them.

Prep Time: 40 minutes

Serving: 6

Ingredients:

- 3 pounds chicken wings, washed and patted dry
- 2 cups barbecue sauce
- ¼ cup bourbon
- 1 teaspoon brown sugar
- 1 teaspoon salt
- 1 teaspoon black pepper
- 1 teaspoon chicken seasoning

Instructions:

1. Combine barbecue sauce, bourbon, brown sugar, salt and pepper in a medium bowl.

2. Season chicken wings with chicken seasoning and place in a large slow cooker and pour barbecue mixture over them and stir until coated.

3. Cook in a slow cooker for 2 ½ to 3 hours.

4. Line two baking sheets with parchment paper and place wings unto them.

5. Heat oven or broiler and cook for 5 - 10 minutes until crispy.

Crispy Fried Chicken Wings

These crispy wings are lightly seasoned and fried to perfection. I personally like mine on the spicy side, so I add some cayenne but this is optional.

Prep Time: 20 minutes

Serving: 6

Ingredients:

- 3 pounds chicken wings, washed and patted dry
- 1 tablespoon chicken seasoning
- 2 teaspoons onion powder
- 2 teaspoons garlic powder
- 1 teaspoon oregano
- 1 teaspoon cayenne (optional)
- 1 teaspoon salt
- 1 teaspoon black pepper
- 2 ½ cups all-purpose flour
- Vegetable oil for frying

Instructions:

1. Season wings with garlic powder, onion powder. Oregano, cayenne, paprika, black pepper and salt. Rest for at least 15 minutes.

2. Mix flour with chicken seasoning in a shallow bowl or plate.

3. Heat at least 2 inches of oil in a large deep pot until shimmering.

4. Working with one wing at a time, coat chicken with flour on all sides and fry until golden and cooked through.

5. Place on a rack or paper towel to drain oil.

Sweet Chili Glazed BBQ Chicken Wings

These juicy chicken wings are covered with tasty sweet chili sauce and barbecue sauce. With this flavor combination, I guarantee you'll not want to put them down.

Prep Time: 40 minutes

Serving: 6

Ingredients:

- 3 pounds of chicken wings, washed and patted dry
- ½ cup ketchup
- ¼ cup brown sugar
- 1 teaspoon honey
- 2 teaspoons chili powder
- 1 teaspoon onion powder
- ½ teaspoon crushed red pepper flakes
- 1 teaspoon chili paste
- ½ teaspoon cayenne pepper
- ⅛ teaspoon ground cinnamon
- 2 tablespoons chili-garlic sauce
- 2 tablespoons garlic, minced
- 2 tablespoons ginger, minced
- 3 tablespoons soy sauce
- ¼ cup olive oil
- 1 teaspoon salt
- 1 teaspoon black pepper

Instructions:

1. Whisk together ketchup, sugar, honey, chili powder, onion powder, red pepper, chili paste, cayenne pepper, cinnamon, chili-garlic sauce, garlic, ginger, soy sauce and olive oil in a large bowl. Reserve ¼ of the mixture for glaze.

2. Add chicken wings to a separate bowl, toss them with salt and pepper and allow them to marinate for at least 20 minutes.

3. Heat grill to medium heat, add chicken wings and cook for about 10 minutes on each side until cooked through and crisp, basting and turning occasionally.

Spicy Maple Chicken Wings

These wings are the perfect balance of a little spicy and a little sweet. They go great with mashed potatoes - or simply on their own!

Prep Time: 40 minutes

Serving: 6

Ingredients:

- 3 pounds chicken wings, washed and patted dry
- ½ cup barbecue sauce
- ¼ cup maple syrup
- 2 tablespoons apple cider vinegar
- 2 tablespoons brown sugar
- 1 teaspoon crushed red pepper flakes

Instructions:

1. Preheat your oven to 450 degrees F.

2. In a medium bowl combine apple cider vinegar, maple syrup, barbecue sauce, brown sugar and red pepper flakes.

3. Brush wings with sauce and place on a parchment lined baking sheet.

4. Bake wings for 30 - 40 minutes until crispy and flip them half way through (15 minutes).

Garlic Parmesan Chicken Wings

Yum! Yes, you read it right! We've blended the delicious flavors of garlic and parmesan and marinated them into crispy chicken wings.

Prep Time: 40 minutes

Serving: 6

Ingredients:

- 3 pounds chicken wings, washed and patted dry
- ¼ cup olive oil
- 1 teaspoon salt
- 1 teaspoon black pepper
- ¼ cup butter, melted
- 2 tablespoons garlic, minced
- 2 teaspoons red pepper flakes
- 1 cup parmesan, freshly grated

Instructions:

1. Preheat your oven to 450 degrees F and place a metal rack over a baking sheet lined with foil.

2. Season wings with olive oil, salt and black pepper. Add to a metal rack and bake until golden and cooked through, about 40 minutes, flipping halfway through.

3. In a large bowl, combine butter, garlic, red pepper flakes and parmesan. When wings are finished, toss them in the garlic parmesan sauce.

Boozy Chicken Wings

Liquor and wings are the perfect pair wherever you go, so why not make your wings boozy from the get?

Prep Time: 40 minutes

Serving: 6

Ingredients:

- 3 pounds of chicken wings, washed and patted dry
- 2 tablespoons of ketchup
- ¼ cup olive oil
- ½ cup brown sugar
- 1 cup coconut liquor
- ¼ cup soy sauce
- 1 small onion, minced
- 2 tablespoons honey
- 1 tablespoon garlic, minced
- 4 yellow habanero peppers, minced
- 1 teaspoon onion powder
- 1 teaspoon salt
- 1 teaspoon black pepper

Instructions:

1. Preheat your oven to 450 degrees F.

2. In a medium bowl combine olive oil, brown sugar, coconut liquor, honey, soy sauce, ketchup, onion, garlic and habanero peppers.

3. Toss chicken wings with onion powder, salt and black pepper.

4. Brush wings with sauce and place on a parchment lined baking sheet.

5. Bake wings for 30 - 40 minutes until crispy and flip them half way through (15 minutes).

Chili Lime Beer Chicken Wings

Another set of boozy wings, but this time, I use beer! The flavors are tied together with tart lime juice and spicy chili!

Prep Time: 40 minutes

Serving: 6

Ingredients:

- 3 pounds chicken wings, washed and patted dry
- 2 cups of pale ale
- 4 tablespoons tomato paste
- ¼ cup fresh lime juice
- ¼ cup honey
- 2 tablespoons soy sauce
- 3 tablespoons red chili sauce
- 2 tablespoons chili powder
- 1 teaspoon salt
- 1 teaspoon black pepper
- 1 teaspoon paprika
- 1 teaspoon garlic powder

Instructions:

1. Combine beer, tomato paste, lime juice, honey, soy sauce, red chili sauce, chili powder, salt, black pepper, paprika and garlic powder.

2. Pour over chicken wings and toss until fully coated. Marinate for at least 20 minutes.

3. Preheat the oven to 450 degrees F. Add wings to an aluminum foil lined baking sheet.

4. Cook wings for 30 - 40 minutes, turning half way through. Brush with remaining marinade while cooking.

Cilantro Lime Wings

If you love the tangy flavor of lime and cilantro, you'll definitely love these Cilantro Lime Wings. All you need are a few ingredients and a few minutes.

Prep Time: 50 minutes

Serving: 6

Ingredients:

- 3 pounds chicken wings, washed and patted dry
- ¼ cup olive oil
- 2 tablespoons lime juice
- 2 tablespoons chopped cilantro
- 2 tablespoons honey
- 1 teaspoon paprika
- 1 teaspoon garlic powder
- 1 tablespoon hot sauce
- 1 teaspoon salt
- 1 teaspoon pepper

Instructions:

1. In a large bowl, mix together olive oil, lime juice, honey, paprika, garlic powder, hot sauce, salt, pepper and cilantro in a bowl.

2. Add chicken wings to the bowl and allow to marinate for at least 20 minutes.

3. Heat your outdoor or indoor grill to medium heat.

4. Add wings to the grill and cook for about 10 minutes each side, until wings are cooked and crisp.

Jerk Chicken Wings

Enjoy a taste of the islands with this mouthwatering spiced jerk chicken dish. These wings are not only spicy but they have a complex flavor profile filled with green onions, garlic, and herbs.

Prep Time: 40 minutes

Serving: 4

Ingredients:

- 3 pounds of chicken wings, washed and patted dry
- ½ cup of olive oil
- 1 medium white onion, minced
- 1 bunch green onions, thinly sliced
- ½ scotch bonnet / 1 medium jalapeno pepper, finely chopped
- 4 garlic cloves, minced
- 1 teaspoon ground allspice
- 1 teaspoon cayenne pepper
- 1 tablespoon fresh ginger, minced
- ¼ cup fresh lime juice
- 2 tablespoons honey
- 2 teaspoons dried thyme
- 1 tablespoon chicken seasoning
- 1 teaspoon salt
- 1 teaspoon black pepper

Instructions:

1. Mix together all of the ingredients except chicken wings in a large bowl.

2. Add chicken wings and marinate for at least 20 minutes.

3. Heat your outdoor or indoor grill to medium heat.

4. Add wings to the grill and cook for about 10 - 15 minutes each side, until wings are cooked and crisp.

Pineapple Chicken Wings

These wings are the perfect blend of sweet and savory. Pineapples add a great sweetness and acidity that make the wings tender and delicious.

Prep Time: 40 minutes

Serving: 6

Ingredients:

- 3 pounds chicken wings, washed and patted dry
- ¼ cup pineapple juice
- 2 cups pineapple chunks
- 1 cup barbecue sauce
- 1 tablespoon brown sugar
- 1 teaspoon onion powder
- 1 teaspoon garlic powder
- 1 teaspoon chicken seasoning
- ¼ cup olive oil
- 1 tablespoon water

Instructions:

1. Preheat your oven to 450 degrees F.

2. Toss wings with olive oil, onion powder, garlic powder and chicken seasoning and place on a parchment lined baking sheet.

3. Bake wings for 20 - 30 minutes and flip them half way through (10 minutes).

4. While your wings are baking, add pineapple juice, pineapple chunks, barbecue sauce, brown sugar and water to a skillet. Cook on low heat until sauce has reduced and thickened.

5. Once wings are ready, remove them from the oven and add to the sauce.

6. Cook over medium heat until sauce has stuck to the wings.

Super Spicy Chicken Wings

Here are the perfect wings for your next spicy wing challenge! Let's see who can handle all this heat.

Prep Time: 40 minutes

Serving: 6

Ingredients:

- 3 pounds chicken wings, washed and patted dry
- ¼ cup olive oil
- ¼ cup hot sauce
- 2 tablespoons crushed red pepper flakes
- 1 tablespoon cayenne
- 1 tablespoon chili powder
- 1 tablespoon paprika
- 1 teaspoon salt
- 1 teaspoon black pepper

Instructions:

1. Preheat your oven to 450 degrees F.

2. In a medium bowl combine olive oil, hot sauce, red pepper flakes, cayenne, chili powder, paprika, salt and pepper.

3. Brush wings with sauce and place on a parchment lined baking sheet.

4. Bake wings for 30 - 40 minutes until crispy and flip them half way through (15 minutes).

Baked Chicken Wings

These baked chicken wings are covered with a delicious spice blend and baked to crispy, juicy perfection.

Prep Time: 40 minutes

Serving: 4

Ingredients:

- 3 pounds chicken wings, washed and patted dry
- ½ cup brown sugar
- 2 tablespoons paprika
- 1 tablespoon garlic powder
- 1 tablespoon onion powder
- 1 teaspoon cumin
- ½ teaspoon cayenne
- 2 teaspoons black pepper
- 1 teaspoon salt
- Cooking spray / vegetable oil

Instructions:

1. Preheat your oven to 450 degrees F. Line a sheet pan with aluminum foil and coat with cooking spray or vegetable oil.

2. In a medium bowl toss chicken wings with brown sugar, paprika, garlic powder, onion powder, cumin, cayenne, black pepper and salt.

3. Place wings on a parchment lined baking sheet.

4. Bake wings for 30 - 40 minutes until crispy and flip them half way through (15 minutes).

Lemon Pepper Chicken Wings

For these wings, I made an easy lemon pepper butter sauce that is brushed over fried chicken wings. This makes sure that you will enjoy crispy wings with delicious flavor.

Prep Time: 40 minutes

Serving: 6

Ingredients:

- Crispy Fried Chicken Wings (Recipe 10)
- ¼ cup butter, melted
- 2 tablespoons lemon pepper seasoning

Instructions:

1. Prepare Crispy Fried Chicken Wings as directed in recipe 10 of this book.

2. Mix butter with lemon pepper seasoning and brush over chicken wings.

3. Toss until well coated.

Honey-Lime Chicken Wings

These wings are a delectable combination of citrus and honey sweetness. This recipe also has a little sriracha and cajun seasoning to give it a spicier flavor.

Prep Time: 40 minutes

Serving: 6

Ingredients:

- 3 pounds chicken wings, washed and patted dry
- 3 tablespoons honey
- 2 tablespoons fresh lime juice
- 1 tablespoon lime zest
- ¼ cup olive oil
- 1 tablespoon Sriracha
- 2 tablespoons Cajun seasoning

Instructions:

1. Mix together all of the ingredients except chicken wings in a large bowl.

2. Add chicken wings and marinate for at least 20 minutes.

3. Heat your outdoor or indoor grill to medium heat.

4. Add wings to the grill and cook for about 10 - 15 minutes each side, until wings are cooked and crisp.

Balsamic Glazed Wings

I definitely recommend these wings for group gatherings. Deliciously sweet and tart and seasoned perfectly.

Prep Time: 30 minutes

Serving: 6

Ingredients:

- 3 pounds chicken wings, washed and patted dry
- ¼ cup olive oil
- 1 tablespoon Italian seasoning
- 1 ¼ cup balsamic vinegar
- ¼ cup honey
- 5 cloves of garlic, minced
- 1 teaspoon salt
- 1 teaspoon black pepper

Instructions:

1. Preheat your oven to 450 degrees F and place a metal rack over a baking sheet lined with foil.

2. Season wings with olive oil, salt and black pepper. Add to a metal rack and bake until golden and cooked through, about 40 minutes, flipping halfway through.

3. In a skillet over medium heat, combine Italian seasoning, balsamic vinegar, honey and garlic. When wings are finished, toss them in the balsamic vinegar sauce.

4. Cook for an additional 2 - 5 minutes until the sauce has thickened.

Italian Style Grilled Chicken Wings

For these wings, I combine signature Italian herbs and spices to make these deliciously seasoned wings.

Prep Time: 40 minutes

Serving: 6

Ingredients:

- 3 pounds chicken wings, washed and patted dry
- ¼ cup olive oil
- 4 garlic cloves, minced
- 3 tablespoons lemon juice
- 1 tablespoon Italian seasoning
- 1 teaspoon garlic powder
- 2 teaspoons onion powder
- 2 teaspoons dried thyme
- 1 teaspoon salt
- 1 teaspoon black pepper

Instructions:

1. In a medium bowl, mix together olive oil, garlic, lemon juice, Italian seasoning, garlic powder, onion powder, thyme, salt and pepper.

2. To marinate chicken wings, place them in a large bowl or a resealable bag with the olive oil mixture. Marinate for at least 20 minutes.

3. Heat your outdoor or indoor grill to medium heat.

4. Add wings to the grill and cook for about 10 - 15 minutes each side, until wings are cooked and crisp.

Spicy Jalapeno Grilled Chicken Wings

These wings are for the spicy lovers! A delightful combination of jalapenos, hot sauce, and chili powder.

Prep Time: 40 minutes

Serving: 4

Ingredients:

- 3 pounds chicken wings, washed and patted dry
- ¼ cup olive oil
- 2 teaspoons lime juice
- ½ cup ketchup
- 2 teaspoons brown sugar
- ¼ cup pickled jalapenos, finely minced
- 2 tablespoons hot sauce
- 2 teaspoons chili powder
- 1 teaspoon garlic powder
- ½ teaspoon cumin
- 1 teaspoon salt
- 1 teaspoon black pepper

Instructions:

1. Mix together olive oil, lime juice, ketchup, brown sugar, jalapenos, hot sauce and salt and pepper. Save ½ cup of the mixture to be used as a glaze.

2. Season wings with garlic powder, cumin and chili powder. Toss wings with the remaining ½ of the mixture and marinate for at least 20 minutes.

3. Preheat your oven to 450 degrees F.

4. Place wings on a wire rack and bake wings for 30 - 40 minutes, turning them half way through.

5. While your wings are baking, add the other ½ of jalapeno sauce to a skillet and cook on low heat until sauce has reduced and thickened.

6. Once wings are ready, remove them from the oven and add to the sauce.

7. Cook over medium heat until sauce has stuck to the wings.

Jack Daniel's Barbecue Wings

These wings will be a definite game changer. People will be asking for more.

Prep Time: 35 minutes

Serving: 6

Ingredients:

- 3 pounds chicken wings, washed and patted dry
- ¼ cup olive oil
- 1 small yellow onion, minced
- 2 ½ cups ketchup
- 1.4 cup molasses
- ¼ cup apple cider vinegar
- ½ cup brown sugar
- 2 tablespoons tomato paste
- ¼ cup Worcestershire sauce
- 1 cup Jack Daniel's whiskey
- 1 teaspoon salt
- 1 teaspoon black pepper

Instructions:

1. Preheat your oven to 450 degrees F. Line a sheet pan with aluminum foil and coat with cooking spray or vegetable oil.

2. In a medium bowl toss chicken wings with olive oil, yellow onion, ketchup, molasses, apple cider vinegar, brown sugar, tomato paste, Worcestershire sauce, Jack Daniel's whiskey, salt and pepper.

3. Place wings on a parchment lined baking sheet.

4. Bake wings for 30 - 40 minutes until crispy and flip them half way through (15 minutes).

Honey Barbecue Chicken Wings

All you need for these sweet, magnificent wings are just five ingredients! Enjoy them in no time.

Prep Time: 35 minutes

Serving: 6

Ingredients:

- 3 pounds chicken wings, washed and patted dry
- 2 cups barbecue sauce
- ½ cup honey
- 1 tablespoon chicken seasoning
- 1 teaspoon chili powder

Instructions:

1. Preheat your oven to 450 degrees F. Line a sheet pan with aluminum foil and coat with cooking spray or vegetable oil.

2. In a medium bowl toss chicken wings with barbecue sauce, honey, chicken seasoning and chili powder.

3. Place wings on a parchment lined baking sheet.

4. Bake wings for 30 - 40 minutes until crispy and flip them half way through (15 minutes).

Cherry Barbecue Chicken Wings

These grilled wings are covered with sweet, tart cherry preserves and spicy habaneros.

Prep Time: 40 minutes

Serving: 6

Ingredients:

- 3 pounds chicken wings, washed and patted dry
- ½ cup cherry preserves
- 2 tablespoons barbecue sauce
- 1 small yellow onion, minced
- 1 large habanero, minced
- 1 teaspoon salt
- 1 teaspoon black pepper

Instructions:

1. Preheat your oven to 450 degrees F. Line a sheet pan with aluminum foil and coat with cooking spray or vegetable oil.

2. In a medium bowl toss chicken wings with barbecue sauce, cherry preserves, yellow onion, habanero, salt and pepper.

3. Place wings on a parchment lined baking sheet.

4. Bake wings for 30 - 40 minutes until crispy and flip them half way through (15 minutes).

Chicken Parm Wings

Chicken Parm just got better! Enjoy these bite-sized versions of your favorite dish.

Prep Time: 40 minutes

Serving: 6

Ingredients:

- 3 pounds chicken wings, washed and patted dry
- 3 cups Italian bread crumbs
- 1 cup freshly grated Parmesan
- 1 teaspoon salt
- 1 teaspoon black pepper
- 3 cups traditional tomato sauce, divided into 2

Instructions:

1. Preheat the oven to 450 degrees F.

2. In a medium bowl combine bread crumbs, parmesan, salt and black pepper. Reserve ½ of the tomato sauce for dipping and one for dredging.

3. Working with 1 wing at a time, dredge it in tomato sauce, shake off excess and coat with bread crumb mixture.

4. Place wings on a baking rack over a baking sheet lined with foil.

5. Bake wings for about 35 - 40 minutes, until cooked through. Turning half way through.

6. Serve with remaining tomato sauce for dipping.

Honey Balsamic Grilled Chicken Wings

These wings are scrumptious because of the sweet tart taste of the balsamic vinegar and sweetness of honey. Completely delicious on their own.

Prep Time: 40 minutes

Serving: 4

Ingredients:

- 3 pounds chicken wings, washed and patted dry
- ¼ cup olive oil
- ½ cup honey
- 2 tablespoons brown sugar
- ½ cup balsamic vinegar
- 2 tablespoons grated fresh ginger
- 1 teaspoon lemon juice
- 1 tablespoon orange juice
- 1 teaspoon orange zest
- 1 teaspoon chicken seasoning
- 1 teaspoon salt
- 1 teaspoon black pepper

Instructions:

1. Mix together olive oil, honey, brown sugar, balsamic vinegar, ginger, lemon juice, orange juice and orange zest.

2. Season wings with chicken seasoning, salt and black pepper. Toss wings with the remaining ½ of the honey balsamic mixture and marinate for at least 20 minutes.

3. Preheat your oven to 450 degrees F.

4. Place wings on a wire rack and bake wings for 30 - 40 minutes, turning them half way through.

5. While your wings are baking, add the other ½ of the sauce to a skillet and cook on low heat until sauce has reduced and thickened.

6. Once wings are ready, remove them from the oven and add to the sauce.

7. Cook over medium heat until sauce has stuck to the wings.

Conclusion

So, what are you waiting for? Dust off your grill or clean out your oven and get started! You can enjoy scrumptious, crispy, flavorful wings in no time. Whether you like them spicy, sweet, a little bit tangy, or a little bit of everything, these recipes will definitely win you over.

No matter when you make them or who you serve them to, they will be a hit!

Author's Afterthoughts

I can't find the perfect words to tell you how grateful I am that you gave this book a chance. I know it must not have been easy seeking this book out and going for it, especially since there are multitudes of materials out there with related content.

You bought the book, but you didn't stop there. You continued, took this journey with me, and read every page back to back. I have to say, you make all this worth it.

I would like to know your thoughts about this book too. Your comments may also help others who are yet to download this book make a decision. What's better than one person reading a book? Two people reading it.

For my new books, follow my author page at http://www.graceberry.net

Thank you,

Grace Berry

About the Author

Grace Berry started as a book reviewer after she graduated from college with a degree in creative writing. Afterward, she worked as an editor for a local magazine. She resigned her post and opted to work as a freelance journalist, writing for newspapers and magazines, online and offline.

On one of such assignments, she wrote content for a food blog – a gig she found interesting. Excited about her discovery, she delved deeper into the food world, rediscovering her concept of food. She took a break from freelancing and sought local restaurateurs and chefs out to gather everything she could about their processes and cooking methods; an encounter she documented and wrote about later.

Grace figured out that she could combine her flair for writing with her newfound love for everything food, so she took a plunge and started writing about recipes and other information related to getting the best from the kitchen to the dining.

Now, she has compiled some of her years of research and experiment into a single volume of work, combining storytelling with factual information. Grace hopes to do more, and maybe start a catering business or a restaurant of her own in the future. At the moment, though, recipe developer and cookbook writer will have to do.

Made in the USA
Middletown, DE
08 December 2020